Dear God
My Spiritual Journey with God

Dear God

My Spiritual Journey with God

world

©Copyright 2005 World Publishing, Nashville, Tennessee. 37214. www.worldpublishing.com

Unless otherwise noted, Scripture quotations are from THE NEW KING JAMES VERSION. Copyright © 1979, 1980, 1982, Thomas Nelson, Inc. Publishers.

Scripture quotations noted KJV are from the Holy Bible, King James Version.

Scripture quotations noted THE MESSAGE are from *The Message* by Eugene H. Peterson, copyright © 1993, 1994, 1995, 1996, 2000. Used by permission of NavPress Publishing Group. All rights reserved.

Scripture quotations noted CEV are from THE CONTEMPORARY ENGLISH VERSION ©1991 by the American Bible Society. Used by permission.

Scripture quotations noted NCV are from *The Holy Bible,* NEW CENTURY VERSION, ©1987, 1988, 1991 by Word Publishing, Nashville, TN 37214. Used by permission.

Scripture quotations noted NIV are from the HOLY BIBLE, NEW INTERNATIONAL VERSION® copyright © 1973, 1978, 1984 by International Bible Society. Used by permission of Zondervan Publishing House. All rights reserved.

Scripture quotations noted NRSV are from the NEW REVISED STANDARD VERSION of the Bible, copyright © 1989 by the Division of Christian Education of the National Council of The Churches of Christ in the U.S.A. All rights reserved.

Scripture quotations noted NASV are from the NEW AMERICAN STANDARD VERSION of the Bible, Copyright 1960, 1962, 1963, 1968, 1971, 1972, 1973, 1975, 1977, 1995 by The Lockman Foundation. Used by permission.

Scripture quotations noted NLT are from the *Holy Bible, New Living Translation,* copyright © 1996. Used by permission of Tyndale House Publishers, Inc., Wheaton, Illinois 60189. All rights reserved.

No portion of this book may be reproduced, stored in a retrieval system, or transmitted in any form or by any means—electronic, mechanical, photocopy, recording, or any other—except for brief quotation in printed reviews, without the prior permission of the publisher.

ISBN 0-5291-2123-9

Printed in China.
1 2 3 4 5—09 08 07 06 05

Dear God

January 1

God Moves

God moves in a mysterious way,
His wonders to perform;
He plants his footsteps in the sea,
And rides upon the storm.

Deep in unfathomable mines
Of never failing skill,
He treasures up his bright designs,
And works his sovereign will.

Ye fearful saints, fresh courage take,
The clouds ye so much dread
Are big with mercy, and shall break
In blessings on your head.

Judge not the Lord by feeble sense,
But trust him for his grace;
Behind a frowning providence,
He hides a smiling face.

His purposes will ripen fast,
Unfolding every hour;
The bud may have a bitter taste,
But sweet will be the flower.

Blind unbelief is sure to err,
And scan his work in vain;
God is his own interpreter,
And he will make it plain.

—*William Cowper*

JANUARY 2

 Take my yoke upon you and learn from me, for I am gentle and humble in heart, and you will find rest for your souls. For my yoke is easy and my burden is light.

—*Matthew 11:29–30*

January 3

> *All* I have seen teaches me to trust the Creator for all I have not seen.
> —*Ralph Waldo Emerson*

January 4

 Write your plans in pencil but give God the eraser.
—*Unknown*

January 5

No matter what has happened to you or is happening in the world around you, God promises to protect you as you walk with Him. Pray that He will and trust Him to do so.
—*Stormie Omartian*

January 6

> So do not fear, for I am with you; do not be dismayed, for I am your God. I will strengthen you and help you; I will uphold you with my righteous right hand.
>
> —Isaiah 41:10
> NIV

January 7

Faith in God is like believing a man can walk over Niagara Falls on a tightrope while pushing a wheelbarrow. Trust in God is like getting into the wheelbarrow! To believe God can do something miraculous is one thing; to risk his willingness to do it in your life is another.

—*James C. Dobson*

JANUARY 8

 Faith, mighty faith, the promise sees, And looks to God alone; Laughs at impossibilities, And cries it shall be done.
—*Charles Wesley*

JANUARY 9

One can never pay in gratitude; one can pay "in kind" somewhere else in life.

—*Anne Morrow Lindbergh*

January 10

> The LORD will guide you always; he will satisfy your needs in a sun-scorched land and will strengthen your frame.
> —*Isaiah 58:11* NIV

JANUARY 11

> *If you are not as close to God as you used to be, who moved?*
> —Unknown

JANUARY 12

Make it the first daily business to understand some part of the Bible clearly, and then the rest of the day to obey it.
—*John Ruskin*

January 13

 The beginning of anxiety is the end of faith; and the beginning of true faith is the end of anxiety.

—*George Mueller*

January 14

 Begin and end the day with him who is the Alpha and Omega, and if you really experience what it is to love God, you will redeem all the time you can for his more immediate service.
—*Susanna Wesley*

JANUARY 15

Trust in the Lord with all thine heart, and lean not unto thine own understanding. In all thy ways acknowledge Him, and he shall direct thy path.
—Proverbs 3:5–6

JANUARY 16

 May we store up the truths of God's Word in our hearts as much as possible.

—*Billy Graham*

January 17

Allow the Spirit of God to dwell within you; then in his love he will come and make a habitation with you; he will reside in you and live in you.

—*Evagrius of Pontus*

January 18

> God waits for the chances we give him to show his great generosity.
> —John Chrysostom

January 19

Enter into his gates with thanksgiving, and into his courts with praise: be thankful unto him, and bless his name.
—*Psalm 100:4* KJV

JANUARY 20

Before me, even as behind, God is, and all is well.
—*John Greenleaf Whittier*

January 21

> Nothing is or can be accidental with God.
> —Henry Wadsworth Longfellow

January 22

A coincidence is a small miracle where God chose to remain anonymous.

—*Heidi Quade*

January 23

 Walking with God down the avenue of prayer, we acquire something of His likeness, and unconsciously we are become witnesses of His beauty and His grace.

—*E. M. Bounds*

JANUARY 24

> *Give all your worries and cares to God, for he cares about what happens to you.*
> —1 Peter 5:7 NLT

January 25

Where there is great love there are always miracles.
—*Willa Cather*

January 26

I am always content with what happens; for I know that what God chooses is better than what I choose.

—*Epictetus*

January 27

> *God brings men into deep waters not to drown them, but to cleanse them.*
> —John H. Aughey

JANUARY 28

 God opens ways where to human senses there is no way. Ask the help of your higher power. Keep your faith.
—*Catherine Ponder*

January 29

A man's heart plans his way, But the LORD directs his steps.
—*Proverbs 16:9*

January 30

> All of us have seen good come out of disaster . . . the blessing in disguise. When you expect good to come from negativity, it will. What you think about, you bring about.
>
> —*Joyce Duco*

January 31

When I pray, coincidences happen. And when I stop praying, the coincidences stop.

—*William Temple*

FEBRUARY 1

 God not only orders our steps, He orders our stops.
—*George Mueller*

FEBRUARY 2

> Jesus answered, "I am the way and the truth and the life. No one comes to the Father except through me.
> —John 14:6

FEBRUARY 3

 All prayers and hopes are a reaching-out for coincidences.
—*Eric Hoffer*

FEBRUARY 4

 When you are in the furnace, your Father keeps His eye on the clock and His hand on the thermostat. He knows just how much we can take.

—*Warren W. Wiersbe*

FEBRUARY 5

> *Have faith, knowing tomorrow will hold the blessings of God.*
> —Robert Schuller

February 6

Look to the LORD and his strength; seek his face always.
—*1 Chronicles 16:11* NIV

FEBRUARY 7

For God Himself works in our souls, in the deepest depths, taking increasing control as we are progressively willing to be prepared for His wonder.

—*Thomas R. Kelly*

FEBRUARY 8

> *God has two dwellings; one in heaven, and the other in a meek and thankful heart.*
> —Izaak Walton

FEBRUARY 9

 If we were given all we wanted here, our hearts would settle for this world rather than the next.

—*Elisabeth Elliot*

FEBRUARY 10

God only asks that you do your best.

—*Robert Hugh Benson*

FEBRUARY 11

> *Worship is giving God the best that He has given you.*
> —Oswald Chambers

FEBRUARY 12

 Call unto me, and I will answer thee, and show thee great and mighty things, which thou knowest not.

—*Jeremiah 33:3 KJV*

FEBRUARY 13

I'm not where I need to be, but thank God I'm not where I used to be! I'm OK and I'm on my way!

—*Joyce Meyer*

FEBRUARY 14

> *If* God is not first in our thoughts and efforts in the mornings, He will be in last place the rest of the day.
> —E. M. Bounds

February 15

 When you read God's Word, you must constantly be saying to yourself, "It is talking to me, and about me."
—*Soren Kierkegaard*

February 16

For You are my rock and my fortress; Therefore, for Your name's sake, Lead me and guide me.

—*Psalm 31: 3*

February 17

> When all else is gone, God is left, and nothing changes Him.
> —*Hannah Whitall Smith*

FEBRUARY 18

THE PROVIDENCE OF GOD IS THE GREAT PROTECTOR OF OUR LIFE AND USEFULNESS, AND UNDER THE DIVINE CARE WE ARE PERFECTLY SAFE FROM DANGER.

—*Charles Haddon Spurgeon*

February 19

What is required of you is faith and a sincere life, not loftiness of intellect or deep knowledge of the mysteries of God.
—*Thomas à Kempis*
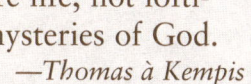

FEBRUARY 20

And when you stand praying, if you hold anything against anyone, forgive him, so that your Father in heaven may forgive you your sins.
—Mark 11:25

FEBRUARY 21

There is always time in a day to do God's will.
—Roy Lessin
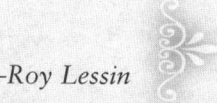

February 22

For every mountain there is a miracle.
—*Robert H. Schuller*
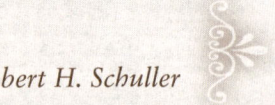

FEBRUARY 23

> *Allow your dreams a place in your prayers and plans. God-given dreams can help you move into the future He is preparing for you.*
> —Barbara Johnson

FEBRUARY 24

 Faith is, then, a lively and steadfast trust in the favor of God, wherewith we commit ourselves altogether unto God.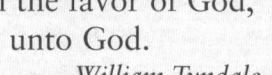
—*William Tyndale*

FEBRUARY 25

 Now this is the confidence that we have in Him, that if we ask anything according to His will, He hears us.
—1 John 5:14

FEBRUARY 26

> *God speaks in the language you know best . . . through your circumstances.*
> —Oswald Chambers

FEBRUARY 27

Life is God's novel. Let him write it.

—*Isaac Bashevis Singer*

FEBRUARY 28

 We are silent at the beginning of the day because God should have the first word, and we are silent before going to sleep because the last word also belongs to God.
—*Dietrich Bonhoeffer*

March 1

> Draw near to God and He will draw near to you.
> —James 4:8

March 2

 God can change our circumstances, but sometimes He waits for us to show real desire for change as well as our faith in Him.

—*Anne Graham Lotz*

March 3

 At the beginning of every act of faith, there is often a seed of fear. For great acts of faith are seldom born out of calm calculation.

—*Max Lucado*

March 4

> God loves us *in* our sin, and *through* our sin, and goes on loving us, looking for a response.
> —Donald Coggan

March 5

 In the day of my trouble I will call upon You, For You will answer me.

—Psalm 86:7

March 6

God is in control, and therefore in everything I can give thanks—not because of the situation but because of the One who directs and rules over it.

—*Kay Arthur*

March 7

 Your talent is God's gift to you. What you do with it is your gift back to God.

—Leo Buscaglia

March 8

> There is nothing we can do to make God love us more. There is nothing we can do to make God love us less.
> —*Philip Yancey*

March 9

I think how much you have helped me; I sing for joy in the shadow of your protecting wings. I follow close behind you; your strong right hand holds me securely.

—*Psalm 63:7–8* NLT

March 10

 To keep the thought of God always in your mind you must cling totally to this formula for piety: "Come to my help, O God; Lord, hurry to my rescue."

—*John Cassian*

March 11

> God can make you everything you want to be, but you have to put everything in his hands.
> —Mahalia Jackson

March 12

 Each day the Lord gives us brings with it a reason to rejoice.
—*Thelma Wells*

March 13

One with God is a majority.

—*Billy Graham*

March 14

> *It is of the Lord's mercies that we are not consumed, because his compassions fail not. They are new every morning: great is thy faithfulness.*
> —*Lamentations 3: 22–23* KJV

March 15

 Faith in small things has repercussions that ripple all the way out. In a huge dark room a little match can light up the place.

—*Joni Eareckson Tada*

March 16

 Be glad that God trusts you with some problems, it is a compliment that He believes you have what it takes to handle them.

—*Norman Vincent Peale*

March 17

Over and over again our spiritual tradition tells us that our will is the part of us which God is interested in, which is needed to fulfill the Kingdom. It is the hardest part of ourselves to commit trustfully, but it is the part of us which is most of use. If we fail to follow our promptings we shall miss God, and God will miss us.

—Margaret Heathfield

March 18

 Blessed are those who keep His testimonies, Who seek Him with the whole heart!

—*Psalm 119:2*

March 19

> Blessed are the single-hearted, for they shall enjoy much peace. If you refuse to be hurried and pressed, if you stay your soul on God, nothing can keep you from that clearness of spirit which is life and peace. In that stillness you will know what His will is.
>
> —Amy Carmichael

March 20

You will build a house for the Lord your God *in and of yourself.* He will be the craftsman, your heart the site, your thoughts the materials. Do not take fright because of your own lack of skill; he who requires this of you is a skillful builder, and he chooses others to be builders, too.
—Hugh of St. Victor

March 21

Everything comes gradually and at its appointed hour.

—*Ovid*

March 22

> Trust in Him at all times, you people; Pour out your heart before Him; God is a refuge for us.
> —Psalm 62:8

March 23

Coincidence is God's way of making His will known.
—*Thomas Aquinas*

March 24

 Cast yourself into the arms of God and be very sure that if He wants anything of you, He will fit you for the work and give you strength.

—*Philip Neri*

March 25

> Man's ultimate destiny is to become one with the Divine Power which governs and sustains the creation and its creatures.
> —*Alfred A. Montapert*

March 26

Do not worry about anything, but pray and ask God for every thing you need, always giving thanks.
—*Philippians 4:6* NCV

March 27

 There are only two kinds of people in the end: those who say to God, "Thy will be done," and those to whom God says, in the end, "Thy will be done."

—C. S. Lewis

March 28

> When God calls you to do something, he enables you to do it.
> —Robert Schuller

March 29

 When we let God's Word seep into our own lives little by little . . . it nourishes us and becomes part of us.
—*Janette Oke*

March 30

Faith sees the invisible, believes the unbelievable, and receives the impossible.

—*Corrie ten Boom*

March 31

> *N*ow faith is the substance of things hoped for, the evidence of things not seen.
> —Hebrews 11:1

April 1

 Open your hearts to the love God instills . . . God loves you tenderly. What He gives you is not to be kept under lock and key, but to be shared.

—*Mother Teresa*

April 2

  Call it Nature, Fate, Fortune; all these are names of the one and selfsame God.

—*Seneca*

April 3

> *Faith is like radar that sees through the fog.*
> —Corrie ten Boom

April 4

 You saw me before I was born. Every day of my life was recorded in your book. Every moment was laid out before a single day had passed.

—*Psalm 139:16* NLT

April 5

 Impossible situations can become possible miracles.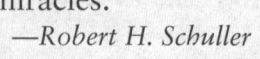
—Robert H. Schuller

April 6

> The more we appropriate God into our lives the more progress we make on the road of Christian godliness and holiness.
> —*Madame Jeanne Guyon*

April 7

To me every hour of the day and night is an unspeakably perfect miracle.

—*Walt Whitman*

April 8

 No eye has seen, no ear has heard, no mind has conceived what God has prepared for those who love Him.
—*1 Corinthians 2:9*

April 9

> *I* think miracles exist in part as gifts and in part as clues that there is something beyond the flat world we see.
> —Peggy Noonan

April 10

Out of difficulties grow miracles.

—*Jean De La Bruyere*

April 11

A Christian is a keyhole through which other folk see God.
—*Robert E. Gibson*

April 12

> So don't worry about tomorrow, for tomorrow will bring its own worries. Today's trouble is enough for today.
> —*Matthew 6:34* CEV

April 13

To be at one with God is to be at peace ... peace is to be found only within, and unless one finds it there he will never find it at all. Peace lies not in the external world. It lies within one's own soul.
—*Ralph W. Trine*

April 14

 Prayer is not monologue, but dialogue; God's voice is its most essential part. Listening to God's voice is the secret of the assurance that He will listen to mine.

—*Andrew Murray*

April 15

All change is a miracle to contemplate; but it is a miracle which is taking place every second.
—*Henry David Thoreau*

April 16

Darkness cannot put out the Light. It can only make God brighter.

—*Unknown*

April 17

 Thy word is a lamp unto my feet, and a light unto my path.
—*Psalm 119:105* KJV

April 18

> *Every morning I spend fifteen minutes filling my mind full of God; and so there's no room left for worry thoughts.*
> —*Howard Chandler Christy*

April 19

 Wash your face every morning in a bath of praise.
—*Charles Haddon Spurgeon*

April 20

 Every morning is a fresh opportunity to find God's extraordinary joy in the most ordinary places.

—*Janet L. Weaver*

April 21

> Praise the Lord. Give thanks to the Lord, for he is good; his love endures forever.
> —Psalm 106:1 NIV

April 22

 God will never, never, never let us down if we have faith and put our trust in Him. He will always look after us. So we must cleave to Jesus. Our whole life must simply be woven into Jesus.
—*Mother Teresa*

April 23

  Faith is taking the first step even when you don't see the whole staircase.

—*Martin Luther King Jr.*

April 24

> See God in every person, place, and thing, and all will be well in your world.
> —*Louise Hay*

April 25

My voice shalt thou hear in the morning, O LORD; in the morning will I direct my prayer unto thee, and will look up.
—*Psalm 5:3*

April 26

Remember, God hears our needs and answers our prayers in the manner that will help us serve his will.

—*Max Lucado*

April 27

I am convinced that many times, in the course of our lives, God challenges us with a golden opportunity, a seemingly impossible hurdle, or a terrible tragedy . . . and how we react—or fail to react—determines the course of our future, almost as if we were involved in some sort of heavenly chess game . . . with our destiny always in the balance.

—*Og Mandino*

April 28

 There is but one thing in the world really worth pursuing—
the knowledge of God.

—*Robert Hugh Benson*

April 29

> The more we depend on God, the more dependable we find he is.
> —Cliff Richard

April 30

Behold, God is my salvation, I will trust and not be afraid; For the LORD GOD is my strength and song, And He has become my salvation.

—*Isaiah 12:2* NASV

May 1

 I have now concentrated all my prayers into one, and that one prayer is this, that I may die to self, and live wholly to him.

—*Charles Haddon Spurgeon*

May 2

> God does not comfort us to make us comfortable, but to make us comforters.
> —*John Henry Jowett*

May 3

> Comfort and prosperity have never enriched the world as much as adversity has.
>
> —*Billy Graham*

May 4

 How the Good God loves those who appreciate the value of his gifts.

—*Julie Billiart*

May 5

Be strong and of good courage, do not fear nor be afraid of them; for the Lord your God, He is the One who goes with you. He will not leave you nor forsake you.

—*Deuteronomy 31:6*

May 6

 All my life I have been looking for a pot of gold at the end of a rainbow, and I found it at the foot of the cross.
—*Dale Evans*

May 7

> God is an unutterable sigh, planted in the depths of the soul.
> —Jean Paul Richter

May 8

 Love is the greatest thing that God can give us, for Himself is love; and it is the greatest thing we can give to God.
—*Jeremy Taylor*

May 9

In the day when I cried out, You answered me, And made me bold with strength in my soul.

—*Psalm 138:3*

May 10

> True humility lies in seeing one's own unworthiness, giving up oneself to God, not doubting for a moment that he can perform the greatest results for us and in us.
>
> —François Fénelon

May 11

God's gifts put man's best dreams to shame.
—*Elizabeth Barrett Browning*

May 12

> Trials teach us what we are; they dig up the soil, and let us see what we are made of.
> —*Charles Haddon Spurgeon*

May 13

 He heals the heartbroken . . . He counts the stars and assigns each a name. Our Lord is great, with limitless strength; we'll never comprehend what He knows and does.

—*Psalm 147:3–5*

May 14

 To place ourselves in range of God's choicest gifts, we have to walk with God, work with God, lean on God, cling to God, come to have the sense and feel of God, refer all things to God.
—*Cornelius Plantinga, Jr.*

May 15

 The stars may fall, but God's promises will stand and be fulfilled.

—*J. I. Packer*

May 16

How will you love Him who so loved you first? Why, in loving Him you will be an imitator of His kindness. And do not marvel that a human being can imitate God. By the will of God he can.

—*Unknown*

May 17

Do all the good you can. By all the means you can. In all the ways you can. In all the places you can. At all the times you can. To all the people you can. As long as ever you can.

—*John Wesley*

May 18

Be not overcome with evil, but overcome evil with good.
—*Romans 12:21*

May 19

 God does not love us because we are valuable. We are valuable because God loves us.

—*Fulton John Sheen*

May 20

I give you praise, O God, for a well-spent day. But I am yet unsatisfied, because I do not enjoy enough of you. I would have my soul more closely united to you by faith and love. I would love you above all things. You, who has made me, know my desires, my expectations. My joys all center in you and it is you yourself that I desire; it is your favor, your acceptance. The communications of your grace I earnestly wish for, more than anything in the world.

—Susanna Wesley

May 21

> Sometimes God doesn't tell us His plan because we wouldn't believe it anyway.
> —*Carlton Pearson*

May 22

Therefore do not be unwise, but understand what the will of the Lord is.

—*Ephesians 5:17*

May 23

I have a great hunger to know God, to learn how to love, to care for the part of my life that is eternal.

—*Sheila Walsh*

May 24

> Start by doing what's necessary; then do what's possible; and suddenly you are doing the impossible.
> —*St. Francis of Assisi*

May 25

 No matter how difficult the challenge, when we spread our wings of faith and allow the winds of God's spirit to lift us, no obstacle is too great to overcome.

—*Roy Lessin*

May 26

Teach me Your way, O Lord; I will walk in Your truth.
—*Psalm 86:11* NASV

May 27

> Are you facing fear today? . . . Don't allow fear to keep you from being used by God. He has kept you thus far; trust Him for the rest of the way.
> —Woodroll Kroll

May 28

 To be grateful is to recognize the love of God in everything He has given us—and He has given us everything. Every breath we draw is a gift of His love.

—*Thomas Merton*

May 29

 Don't believe in miracles—depend on them.

—*Laurence J. Peter*

May 30

> My kindness is all you need. My power is strongest when you are weak.
>
> —*2 Corinthians 12:9* CEV

May 31

Incline us, oh God!, to think humbly of ourselves, to be severe only in the examination of our own conduct, to consider our fellow-creatures with kindness, and to judge of all they say and do with that charity which we would desire from them ourselves.

—*Jane Austen*

June 1

 For the truly faithful, no miracle is necessary. For those who doubt, no miracle is sufficient.
—*Nancy Gibbs*

June 2

Every believer is God's miracle.

—*Philip James Bailey*

June 3

> The search for God is, indeed, an entirely personal undertaking . . . the most audacious adventure that one can dare.
> —Alexis Carrel

June 4

> *L*ove the LORD your God, listen to his voice, and hold fast to him. For the LORD is your life.
> —*Deuteronomy* 30:20 NIV

June 5

 Our real blessings often appear to us in the shape of pains, losses and disappointments.

—*Joseph Addison*

June 6

Have patience with all things, but chiefly have patience with yourself. Do not lose courage in considering your own imperfections but instantly set about remedying them—every day begin the task anew.

—*Francois de Sales*

June 7

 If we use God's talents, we shall find that they become multiplied in the use. We thought we had two; we find we have five.

—*Richard Meux Benson*

June 8

 When I stand before God at the end of my life, I would hope that I would not have a single bit of talent left, and could say, "I used everything you gave me."

—*Erma Bombeck*

June 9

But the fruit of the Spirit is love, joy, peace, patience, kindness, goodness, faithfulness, gentleness, and self-control.
—*Galatians 5:22–23*

June 10

> There are only two ways to live your life. One is as though nothing is a miracle. The other is as though everything is a miracle.
> —Richard Crashaw

June 11

 If I am not in God's grace, may God bring me there; if I am in it, may he keep me there.

—*Joan of Arc*

June 12

 We forget that God is a specialist. He is well able to work our failures into His plans.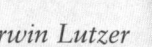

—*Erwin Lutzer*

June 13

> God is our refuge and strength, a very present help in trouble.
> —Psalm 46:1

June 14

The ultimate ground of faith and knowledge is confidence in God.

—*Charles Hodge*

June 15

  We have to pray with our eyes on God, not on the difficulties.
—*Oswald Chambers*

June 16

> Hope is not the conviction that something will turn out well, but the certainty that something makes sense regardless of how it turns out.
> —Barbara Johnson

June 17

 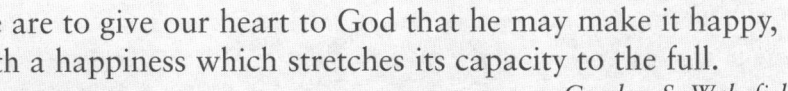

We are to give our heart to God that he may make it happy, with a happiness which stretches its capacity to the full.
—*Gordon S. Wakefield*

June 18

You are my hiding place and my shield; I hope in Your word.
—*Psalm 119:14*

June 19

> *I* believe in the sun even if it isn't shining. I believe in love even when I am alone. I believe in God even when He is silent.
>
> —*Found on a wall in a concentration camp*

June 20

 A firm faith in the universal providence of God is the solution of all earthly troubles.

—B. B. Warfield

June 21

 If we just give God the little that we have, we can trust Him to make it go around.

—*Gloria Gaither*

June 22

So I pray that God, who gives you hope, will keep you happy and full of peace as you believe in him. May you overflow with hope through the power of the Holy Spirit.

—*Romans 15:13* NLT

June 23

He who trusts in himself is lost. He who trusts in God can do all things.

—*Alphonsus Liguori*

June 24

We come closest to God at our lowest moments. It's easiest to hear God when you are stripped of pride and arrogance, when you have nothing to rely on except God. It's pretty painful to get to that point, but when you do, God is there.

—Terry Anderson in *Our Sunday Visitor*

June 25

 Trust the past to God's mercy, the present to God's love, and the future to God's providence.

— *Augustine*

June 26

> *He who gives heed to the word will prosper, and happy is he who trusts in the Lord.*
> —*Proverbs 16:20*
> NRSV

June 27

 To God, our journey is as important as our destination.
—Beth Moore

June 28

The world is crooked and God straightens it.
—*Alexander Elchaninov*

June 29

How do you know if an angel has crossed your path? Sometimes you don't, because angels often appear as coincidences. That is, they seem like chance events, but they are really part of God's carefully orchestrated plan for your life.
—*Gary Kinnaman*, in *Angels Dark and Light*

June 30

 Don't forget to be kind to strangers. For some who have done this have entertained angels without realizing it.
—*Hebrews 13:2*

July 1

> What a mighty thing it is to live for God's kingdom! Live for it; look for it—it is so powerful it will completely overwhelm you.
> —J. Heinrich Arnold

July 2

 Everything that happens is either a blessing which is also a lesson, or a lesson which is also a blessing.
—*Polly Berrien Berends*

July 3

 With the goodness of God to desire our highest welfare, the wisdom of God to plan it, and the power of God to achieve it, what do we lack?

—*A. W. Tozer*

July 4

> *Ask* sk God's blessing on your work, but don't ask him to do it for you.
> —*Dame Flora Robson*

July 5

Cast your cares on the Lord and He will sustain you.
—*Psalm 55:22*

July 6

 God's care for us is more watchful and more tender than the care of any human father could possibly be.
—*Hannah Whitall Smith*

July 7

> We cannot truly face life until we face the fact that it will be taken away from us.
> —*Billy Graham*

July 8

> Come, haste ye away and walk with God . . . there is a heaven at the end of this walk.
>
> —George Whitefield

July 9

 But if from there you seek the Lord your God, you will find him if you look for him with all your heart and all your soul.
—*Deuteronomy 4:29* NIV

July 10

> People see God every day, they just don't recognize him.
> —*Pearl Bailey*

July 11

 Every tomorrow has two handles. We can take hold of it with the handle of anxiety or the handle of faith.
—*Henry Ward Beecher*

July 12

God does not ask your ability or your inability. He asks only your availability.

—*Mary Kay Ash*

July 13

When we have done all we can, we must still wait for God to accomplish His purposes. As we wait, we can fix our eyes on Jesus as a companion who empathizes with our suffering and a Savior who is working behind the scenes. Difficult circumstances seem to increase our ability to experience intimacy with Christ.
—*Ruthann Ridley*

July 14

I tell you the truth, if you have faith as small as a mustard seed, you can say to this mountain, 'Move from here to there' and it will move.

— *Matthew 17:20*

July 15

> God's love sets us truly free. Our love finds its fulfillment in being transformed into God's love, and only then will our works be truly fruitful.
> —*Simon Tugwell*

July 16

 Worshiping in all the moments of our lives changes us because we move from trying to be perfect to resting in the perfect will of a God who loves us passionately.

—*Sheila Walsh*

July 17

I was regretting the past and fearing the future. Suddenly God was speaking: "My name is I am." I waited and God continued: "When you live in the past, with its mistakes and regrets, it is hard. I am not there. My name is not I was. When you live in the future, with its problems and fears, it is hard. I am not there. My name is not I will be. When you live in this moment, it is not hard. I am here. My name is I AM."

—Helen Mellincost

July 18

 God's Word is as good as He is. There is an old saying that a man is as good as his word. Well, God is as good as His Word. His character is behind what He has said.

—J. Vernon McGee

July 19

 So then faith comes by hearing, and hearing by the word of God.

—*Romans 10:17*

July 20

> *I believe the Bible is the best gift God has ever given to man. All the good from the Savior of the world is communicated to us through this book.*
> —Abraham Lincoln

July 21

When you have read the Bible you will know that it is the word of God, because you will have found it the key to your own heart, your own happiness, your own duty.
—*Thomas Woodrow Wilson*

July 22

Adversity is always unexpected and unwelcomed. It is an intruder and a thief, and yet in the hands of God, adversity becomes the means through which His supernatural power is demonstrated.

—Charles Stanley

July 23

The hand of our God is upon all those for good who seek Him, but His power and His wrath are against all those who forsake Him.

—*Ezra 8:22*

July 24

 If we only have the will to walk, then God is pleased with our stumbles.

—*C. S. Lewis*

July 25

> Do not lose faith in God. The grace He gives will be in direct proportion to the amount of sufferings you must bear. No one else can do this except the Creator who made us and knows how to renew our strength by His grace.
>
> —*Francois Fenelon*

July 26

The truth is that our trials are a furnace forging us into gold.
—*Barbara Johnson*

July 27

> *Be* strong and courageous. Do not be terrified; do not be discouraged, for the LORD your God will be with you wherever you go.
> —*Joshua 1:9* NIV

July 28

 Your life is only as productive as the freshness of your walk with God.

—*Randy Shankle*

JULY 29

 Little faith will bring your soul to heaven; great faith will bring heaven to your soul.

—*Unknown*

July 30

When one door closes, another opens. But we often look so long and so regretfully upon the closed door that we fail to see the one that has opened for us.

—*Alexander Graham Bell*

July 31

When we lose God, it is not God who is lost.
—*Unknown*

August 1

Listen to my instruction and be wise; do not ignore it.
—Proverbs 8:33

August 2

When you are in the dark, listen, and God will give you a very precious message.

—*Oswald Chambers*

August 3

Faith is daring the soul to go beyond what the eyes can see.
—*William Newton Clark*

August 4

It's not the rules and regulations you follow carefully that will win you favor with God but rather offering your life to Him in complete faith that His Son, Jesus Christ, conquered sin and death on your behalf and for your salvation.

—*James L. Mathews*

August 5

Have thy tools ready, God will find the work.
—*Charles Kingsley*

August 6

> For the LORD searches all hearts and understands all the intent of the thoughts. If you seek Him, He will be found by you.
> —1 Chronicles 28:9

August 7

 Miracles are not a contradiction of nature. They are only in contradiction of what we know of nature.

—*St. Augustine*

August 8

 Learn to worship God as the God who does wonders, who wishes to prove in you that He can do something supernatural and divine.

—*Andrew Murray*

August 9

> Accept me, Lord, as I am, and make me such as thou wouldst have me be.
> —Mary Livingstone

August 10

O come, let us worship and bow down; let us kneel before the LORD our maker.

—*Psalm 95:6*

August 11

 Even now, two thousand years later, we marvel at the beautiful way God has provided what we need most. Being born again is God's solution to our need for love and life and light.
—*Anne Graham Lotz*

August 12

> God does not desire 'something' from us—he desires us, ourselves, not our works, but our personality, our will, our heart.
> —*Emil Brunner*

August 13

 The purpose of prayer is not to inform God of our needs, but to invite him to rule our lives.
—*Clarence Bauman*

August 14

The center of God's will is our only safety.

—*Betsie ten Boom*

August 15

I trust in the mercy of God for ever and ever.

—*Psalm 52:8*

August 16

> Faith is not belief without proof, but trust without reservation.
> —Elton Trueblood

August 17

> God both represents to us what we are to become and shows us the way to become it.
> —Don Cupitt

August 18

Man is born broken. He lives by mending. The grace of God is glue.

—*Eugene O'Neill*

August 19

In him we have redemption through his blood, the forgiveness of sins, in accordance with the riches of God's grace.
—*Ephesians 1:7*

August 20

 True forgiveness includes total acceptance.
—*Catherine Marshall*

August 21

Praise Him! Praise Him! Jesus our blessed Redeemer. He redeems our souls; He reveals our future; He resolves our problems; He receives our praise. How rich we are since Jesus came our way.

—Robert J. Morgan

August 22

Be assured, if you walk with Him, and look to Him, and expect help from Him, He will never fail you.

—*George Muëller*

August 23

> *In God, whose word I praise, in God I trust; I will not be afraid. What can mortal man do to me?*
> —Psalm 56:4

August 24

 Faith is affirming success before it comes. Faith is making claims to victory before it is achieved.
—*Robert Schuller*

August 25

Everyone has inside of him a piece of good news. The good news is that you don't know how great you can be! How much you can love! What you can accomplish! And what your potential is!
—Anne Frank

August 26

 There should be, even in the busiest day, a few moments when we can close our eyes and let God possess us.
—*Caryll Houselander*

August 27

 What a tremendous relief it should be, and has been to many, to discover that we don't need to prove ourselves to God. We don't have to do anything at all, to be acceptable to Him.
—*Desmond Tutu*

August 28

> A friendly smile makes you happy, and good news makes you feel strong.
> —Proverbs 15:30
> CEV

August 29

God understands our prayers even when we can't find the words to say them.

—*Unknown*

August 30

By living fully, recognizing that all we do is by His power, we honor God; He in turn blesses us.

—*Becky Laird*

August 31

> To us also, through every star, through every blade of grass, is not God made visible if we will open our minds and our eyes.
> —*Thomas Carlyle*

SEPTEMBER 1

Therefore the LORD waits to be gracious to you; therefore he will rise up to show mercy to you. For the LORD is a God of justice; blessed are all those who wait for him.

—*Isaiah 30:18* NRSV

SEPTEMBER 2

 Be kind and merciful. Let no one ever come to you without coming away better and happier. Be the living expression of God's kindness.

—*Mother Teresa*

SEPTEMBER 3

> The Bible is... as necessary to spiritual life as breath is to natural life. There is nothing more essential to our lives than the Word of God.
> —*Jack Hayford*

September 4

God is our true Friend, who always gives us the counsel and comfort we need. Our danger lies in resisting Him; so it is essential that we acquire the habit of hearkening to His voice, or keeping silence within, and listening so as to lose nothing of what He says to us.

—*Francoise Fenelon*

SEPTEMBER 5

May He grant you according to your heart's desire, And fulfill all your purpose.

—*Psalm 20:4*

SEPTEMBER 6

 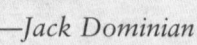 You never lose the love of God. Guilt is the warning that temporarily you are out of touch.

—*Jack Dominian*

September 7

 The purpose of life is to live a life of purpose.

—*Robert Byrne*

September 8

 Faith is deliberate confidence in the character of God whose ways you may not understand at the time.
—*Oswald Chambers*

September 9

> Oh God, though our sins be seven, though our sins be seventy times seven, though our sins be more than the hairs of our head, yet give us grace in loving penitence to cast ourselves down into the depths of thy compassion.
>
> —*Christina Rossetti*

SEPTEMBER 10

 Be still, and know that I am God.

—*Psalm 46:10*

SEPTEMBER 11

 I know the Bible is inspired because it inspires me.
—*Dwight L. Moody*

SEPTEMBER 12

> The Word of God is a powerful sword of an upright man.
> —José B. Cabajar

SEPTEMBER 13

God gives the cross, and the cross gives us God.
—*Madame Jeanne Guyon*

SEPTEMBER 14

 Let the word of Christ dwell in you richly; teach and admonish one another in all wisdom; and with gratitude in your hearts sing psalms, hymns, and spiritual songs to God.
—*Colossians 3:16* NRSV

SEPTEMBER 15

> When you can't trace His hand you can trust His heart.
> —*Charles Haddon Spurgeon*

September 16

 You can give without loving, but you cannot love without giving.

—*Amy Carmichael*

SEPTEMBER 17

 What is Christian perfection? Loving God with all our heart, mind, soul, and strength.

—*John Wesley*

September 18

In all this I have given you an example that by such work we must support the weak, remembering the words of the Lord Jesus, for he himself said, "It is more blessed to give than to receive."

—*Acts 20:35* NRSV

SEPTEMBER 19

 God hath given to man a short time here upon earth, and yet upon this short time eternity depends.

—*Jeremy Taylor*

September 20

In the midst of the awesomeness, a touch comes, and you know it is the right hand of Jesus Christ. You know it is not the hand of restraint, correction, nor chastisement, but the right hand of the Everlasting Father. Whenever His hand is laid upon you, it gives inexpressible peace and comfort, and the sense that "underneath are the everlasting arms" (Deuteronomy 33:27) full of support, provision, comfort, and strength.

—Oswald Chambers

SEPTEMBER 21

 Faith is seeing the invisible, but not the nonexistent.
—A. W. Tozer

SEPTEMBER 22

> *I* can get more out of God by believing Him for one minute than I can by shouting at Him all night.
> —*Smith Wigglesworth*

September 23

We know that all things work together for good to them that love God, to them who are the called according to his purpose.

—*Romans 8:28*

SEPTEMBER 24

Destiny has two ways of crushing us—by refusing our wishes and by fulfilling them. But he who only wills what God wills escapes both catastrophes. All things work together for his good.
—*Elisabeth Elliot*

SEPTEMBER 25

> As I understand the meaning of the word "faith," it means that I am content not to understand certain things in this life.
> —*Martyn Lloyd-Jones*

SEPTEMBER 26

 Who but God can set men free? And He sets them free as they walk with Him.

—*Andrew Jukes*

SEPTEMBER 27

I am your servant; give me understanding, that I may know your testimonies.

—*Psalm 119:125*

September 28

 God raises the level of the impossible.

—*Corrie ten Boom*

SEPTEMBER 29

Were the works of God readily understandable by human reason, they would be neither wonderful nor unspeakable.
—Thomas a Kempis

September 30

There come times when I have nothing more to tell God. If I were to continue to pray in words, I would have to repeat what I have already said. At such times it is wonderful to say to God, "May I be in Thy presence, Lord? I have nothing more to say to Thee, but I do love to be in Thy presence."

—O. Hallesby

October 1

How many are your works, O Lord! In wisdom you made them all; the earth is full of your creatures. There is the sea, vast and spacious, teeming with creatures beyond number—living things both large and small.

—*Psalm 104:24–25*

October 2

God's love and power and faithfulness are the same, whether he deals with women or with men.

—*Florence Booth*

OCTOBER 3

> Every happening, great and small, is a parable whereby God speaks to us, and the art of life is to get the message.
> —*Malcolm Muggeridge*

OCTOBER 4

> Faith is the first factor in a life devoted to service. Without it, nothing is possible. With it, nothing is impossible.
> —*Mary McLeod Bethune*

October 5

 Communion with God is a relationship, not a sensation.
—*Bruce Wilkinson*

October 6

As for me and my house, we will serve the Lord.

—Joshua 24:15

OCTOBER 7

Prayer is kind of like calling home every day.
—*Barbara Johnson*

OCTOBER 8

The longer I live, the more convincing proofs I see of this truth: that God governs in the affairs of men. And if a sparrow cannot fall to the ground without His notice, is it probable that an empire can rise without his aid?

—Benjamin Franklin

October 9

 God gives when he will, as he will and to whom he will.
—*Teresa of Avila*

OCTOBER 10

> *Are not two sparrows sold for a copper coin? And not one of them falls to the ground apart from your Father's will.*
> —Matthew 10:29

October 11

God of our life, there are days when the burdens we carry chafe our shoulders and weigh us down; when the road seems dreary and endless, the skies grey and threatening; when our lives have no music in them, and our hearts are lonely, and our souls have lost their courage. Flood the path with light, run our eyes to where the skies are full of promise; tune our hearts to brave music; give us the sense of comradeship with heroes and saints of every age; and so quicken our spirits that we may be able to encourage the souls of all who journey with us on the road of life, to Your honor and glory.
—*Augustine*

October 12

You must live with people to know their problems, and live with God in order to solve them.

—*Peter Taylor Forsyth*

OCTOBER 13

> *God gives us fresh mercy each morning—enough to get through one day at a time.*
> —Sheila Walsh

OCTOBER 14

 Have courage for the great sorrows of life and patience for the small ones. And when you have finished your daily task, go to sleep in peace. God is awake.

—*Victor Hugo*

October 15

Those that wait upon the LORD shall renew their strength.
—*Isaiah 40:31*

October 16

> The times we find ourselves having to wait on others may be the perfect opportunities to train ourselves to wait on the Lord.
> —Joni Eareckson Tada

October 17

 We can walk without fear, full of hope and courage and strength . . . waiting for the endless good which God is always giving as fast as He can get us to take it in.
—*George MacDonald*

October 18

The person you are now, the person you have been, the person you will yet be—*this* person God has chosen as beloved.
—*William Countryman*

October 19

> God is love, and he who abides in love abides in God, and God in him.
> —1 John 4:16 NASV

October 20

 God would be pleased if you were to take one last look in the mirror before you start your day and say, "God loves you . . . and so do I."

—Zig Ziglar

October 21

To have God speak to the heart is a majestic experience, an experience that people may miss if they monopolize the conversation and never pause to hear God's responses.
—*Charles Stanley*

OCTOBER 22

Because of Christ's resurrection—and His guarantee that He will resurrect all who believe in Him—we are the most fortunate, the most blest people on the planet! Our faith is effective, we are not in our sins, our departed loved ones are with the Lord, and the labor we do for Him is not in vain.

—*Bob Wilkin*

October 23

The LORD is my light and my salvation; whom shall I fear?
The LORD is the strength of my life; of whom shall I
be afraid?

—*Psalm 27:1*

October 24

 Nothing can make a man truly great but being truly good and partaking of God's holiness.

—*Matthew Henry*

October 25

We get new ideas from God every hour of our day when we put our trust in Him—but we have to follow that inspiration up with perspiration—we have to work to prove our faith. Remember that the bee that hangs around the hive never gets any honey.
—*Albert E. Cliffe*

OCTOBER 26

> Love him totally who gave himself totally for your love.
> —*Clare of Assisi*

October 27

Happiness is to be found only in the home where God is loved and honored where each one loves, and helps, and cares for the others.

—*Theophanes Vénard*

OCTOBER 28

 Seek first the kingdom of God and His righteousness, and all these things shall be added to you.

—*Matthew 6:33*

October 29

> *Faith is the conviction that God knows more than we do about this life and He will get us through it.*
> —*Max Lucado*

October 30

 "What do you think of God," the teacher asked. After a pause, the young pupil replied, "He's not a think, he's a feel."

—*Paul Frost*

OCTOBER 31

What is faith? It is being fully persuaded that God has the power to do what He has promised.
—*Robert J. Morgan*

November 1

By faith we have been made acceptable to God. And now, because of our Lord Jesus Christ, we live at peace with God.
—*Romans 5:1* CEV

November 2

God's promise to the pure of heart is of that knowledge of himself through love which is eternal life; and the heart will be pure when it is filled with the love of God 'in all things and above all things.' To be filled with such love is to have obtained the promises which exceed all that we can desire.

—*John Burnaby*

November 3

> Were there no God, we would be in this glorious world with grateful hearts and no one to thank.
> —*Christina Rossetti*

November 4

  If we give our whole life to God, holding nothing back He will give His whole life to us, holding nothing back.
—*Sam Haney*

November 5

 Uphold my steps in Your paths, That my footsteps may not slip.

—*Psalm 17:5*

November 6

What you need to do, is to put your will over completely into the hands of your Lord, surrendering to Him the entire control of it. Say, "Yes, Lord, YES!" to everything, and trust Him to work in you.

—*Hannah Whitall Smith*

November 7

If you wish to possess finally all that is yours, give yourself entirely to God.

—*Hadewijch of Brabant*

November 8

> Faith is to believe what you do not yet see; the reward for this faith is to see what you believe.
> —*St. Augustine*

November 9

 Walk boldly and wisely. . . . There is a hand above that will help you on.

—*Philip James Bailey*

November 10

Guide my steps by your word, so I will not be overcome by any evil.

—*Psalm 119:133* NLT

November 11

 Nothing hath separated us from God but our own will, or rather our own will is our separation from God.
—*William Law*

November 12

For a long time it had seemed to me that life was about to begin—real life. But there are always some obstacles in the way, something to be gotten through first, some unfinished business, time still to be served, a debt to be paid. Then life would begin. At last it dawned on me that these obstacles were my life.

—*Alfred D. Souza*

November 13

> Two men please God—who serves Him with all his heart because he knows Him; who seeks Him with all his heart because he knows Him not.
> —*Nikita Ivanovich Panin*

November 14

 Be of good comfort, be of one mind, live in peace; and the God of love and peace will be with you.

—*2 Corinthians 13:11*

November 15

 God is trying to get a message through to you, and the message is: "Stop depending on inadequate human resources. Let me handle the matter."

—*Catherine Marshall*

November 16

> We have to choose daily to allow the mind of Christ to be in us and to allow the wisdom of God to guide us.
> —*Stormie Omartian*

November 17

No one is so empty as the man who has stopped walking with God and doesn't know it.

—*Jerry White*

November 18

> I must know that I am walking with God. I must know that I understand the mystery of godliness. I must know that the grace of God is in my own heart, that my own life is in accordance with his will, that I am walking in his footsteps. Then my words will be true, and my actions right.
> —*Ellen G. White*

November 19

 For God so loved the world, that he gave his only begotten Son, that whosoever believeth in him should not perish, but have everlasting life.

—*John 3:16* KJV

November 20

Faith does not, in the realist, spring from miracles, but miracles from faith.

—*Lloyd John Ogilvie*

November 21

It helps me if I remember that God is in charge of my day—not I.

—*Charles R. Swindoll*

November 22

For, after all, put it as we may to ourselves, we are all of us from birth to death guests at a table which we did not spread. The sun, the earth, love, friends, our very breath are parts of the banquet. . . . Shall we think of the day as a chance to come nearer to our Host, and to find out something of Him who has fed us so long?

—*Rebecca Harding Davis*

November 23

> *Yea, though I walk through the valley of the shadow of death, I will fear no evil: for thou art with me; thy rod and thy staff they comfort me.*
> *—Psalm 23:4 KJV*

November 24

 Through prayer, God greatly multiplies our efforts. What we can do on our own is limited, but what God can do is endless.

—*John Maxwell*

November 25

Measure not God's love and favor by your own feeling. The sun shines as clearly in the darkest day as it does in the brightest. The difference is not in the sun, but in some clouds which hinder the manifestation of the light thereof.
—*Richard Sibbes*

November 26

 Prayer is the place of refuge for every worry, a foundation for cheerfulness, a source of constant happiness, a protection against sadness.

—*St. John Chrysostom*

November 27

 Make me walk in the path of Your commandments, For I delight in it.

—*Psalm 119:35*

November 28

> Before God made us, he loved us. This love was never diminished nor ever shall it ever be. And in this love he has done all his work.
> —*Julian of Norwich*

November 29

 Where there is faith, there is love; Where there is love, there is peace; Where there is peace, there is God; And where there is God, there is no need.

—*Leo Tolstoy*

November 30

There is not in the world a kind of life more sweet and delightful than that of a continual walk with God.
—*Brother Lawrence*

December 1

To walk with God, we must talk with God.
—*Unknown*

December 2

I will give peace in the land, and you shall lie down, and none will make you afraid.

—*Leviticus 26:6*

December 3

We must focus on prayer as the main thrust to accomplish God's will and purpose on earth. The forces against us have never been greater and this is the only way we can release God's power to become victorious.

—*John Maxwell*

December 4

> God possesses infinite knowledge and an awareness which is uniquely His. At all times, even in the midst of any type of suffering, I can realize that He knows, loves, watches, understands, and more than that, He has a purpose.
>
> —*Billy Graham*

December 5

God's delay and His ways can be confusing because the process God uses to accomplish His will can go against human logic and common sense. The reason for this is to focus our faith, not in our friends or our abilities or resources or knowledge or strength or anything other than Him alone.

—Anne Graham Lotz

December 6

Now acquaint yourself with Him, and be at peace; Thereby good will come to you.

—*Job 22:21*

December 7

> Day by day, morning by morning, begin your walk with Him in the calm trust that God is at work in everything.
> —*Anne Ortlund,* in *Disciplines of the Heart*

December 8

Walk closer with your God than you have in days past: for the nearer you walk with God, the more you will enjoy of Him whose presence is life.

—*George Whitefield*

December 9

If there are a thousand steps between us and God, he will take all but one. He will leave the final one for us. The choice is ours.

—*Max Lucado*

December 10

> *He ... set my feet upon a rock, And established my steps.*
> —Psalm 40:2

December 11

You shall walk after the LORD your God and fear Him, and keep His commandments and obey His voice; you shall serve Him and hold fast to Him.

—*Deuteronomy 13:4*

December 12

 Whenever you are tempted to the commission of any sin, or the omission of any duty, pause and say to yourself, "What am I about to do? God sees me."

—*Susanna Wesley*

December 13

> My worth to God in public is what I am in private.
> —Oswald Chambers

December 14

Don't think so much about who is for or against you, rather give all your care, that God be with you in everything you do.
—*Thomas á Kempis*

DECEMBER 15

Obey My voice, and I will be your God, and you will be My people; and you will walk in all the ways which I command you, that it may be well with you.

—*Jeremiah 7:23* NASV

December 16

> The Christian is a person who makes it easy for others to believe in God.
> —*Robert M. McCheyne*

December 17

Our lives are full of supposes. Suppose this should happen, or suppose that should happen; what could we do; how could we bear it? But, if we are living in the high tower of the dwelling place of God, all these supposes will drop out of our lives. We shall be quiet from the fear of evil, for no threatenings of evil can penetrate into the high tower of God. Even when walking through the valley of the shadow of death, the psalmist could say, I will fear no evil; and, if we are dwelling in God, we can say so too.

—Hannah Whitall Smith

December 18

Lord, make my life a window for Your light to shine through and a mirror to reflect Your love to all I meet. Amen.
—*Robert Schuller*

December 19

 For we are His workmanship, created in Christ Jesus for good works, which God prepared beforehand so that we would walk in them.

—*Ephesians 2:10* NASV

December 20

Peace is the gift of God. Do you want peace? Go to God.
—*John Taylor*

December 21

> *God grant me the serenity to accept the things I cannot change, the courage to change the things I can, and the wisdom to know the difference.*
> —Serenity Prayer

December 22

If God sends us on stony paths, he provides strong shoes.
—*Corrie ten Boom*

DECEMBER 23

 For the LORD God is a sun and shield; The LORD will give grace and glory; No good thing will He withhold from those who walk uprightly.

—Psalm 84:11

DECEMBER 24

> *Pray. Prayer is the way to listen to God, to speak with Him, to understand His love for us.*
> —*Mother Teresa*

December 25

> Faith is no irresponsible shot in the dark. It is a responsible trust in God, who knows the desires of your hearts, the dreams you are given, and the goals you have set. He will guide your paths right.
>
> —*Robert Schuller*

December 26

 God is everything that is good, in my sight, and the goodness that everything has is His.

—*Julian of Norwich*

December 27

The LORD will give strength to His people; The LORD will bless His people with peace.

—*Psalm 29:11*

December 28

 I would rather walk with God in the dark than go alone in the light.

—*Mary Gardiner Brainard*

December 29

How blessed and amazing are God's gifts, dear friends! Life with immortality, splendor with righteousness, truth with confidence, faith with assurance, self-control with holiness! And all these things are within our comprehension.
—*Clement of Rome*

December 30

 God has given us two hands—one for receiving and the other for giving.

—*Billy Graham*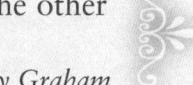

December 31

With God all things are possible.

—*Mark 10:27*

Acknowledgments

Every effort was made to properly attribute all quoted materials in this book. The quotes are not in all cases, exact quotations, as some have been edited for clarity and brevity, but in all cases, an attempt has been made to maintain the speaker's original intent. In some cases quoted material for the book was obtained from secondary sources, including print media and websites. Although every effort was made to ensure the accuracy of the sources and the quotes, it cannot be guaranteed. Grateful acknowledgment is also made to the following for permission to reprint copyrighted material:

Adventurous Prayer © 2003, excerpted by permission of Thomas Nelson Publishers.

Big Wisdom {Little Book} ©2005 excerpted by permission of W Publishing Group, a division of Thomas Nelson Publishers.

Checklist for Life, © 2002 GRQ, Inc., excerpted by permission of Thomas Nelson Publishers.

Checklist for Life for Moms, © 2005 GRQ, Inc., excerpted by permission of Thomas Nelson Publishers.

Checklist for Life for Teachers, © 2005 GRQ, Inc., excerpted by permission of Thomas Nelson Publishers.

Donelson Fellowship, The ©2004, *Pocket Papers,* http://www.donelson.org/pocket.cfm.

Faith for a Lifetime, © 2005 Women of Faith, excerpted by permission of J. Countryman, a division of Thomas Nelson Publishers.

God's Daily Answer, © 2003, excerpted by permission of Elm Hill Books, an imprint of J. Countryman, a division of Thomas Nelson Publishers.

God's Survival Guide for Women, © 2005, excerpted by permission of Elm Hill Books, an imprint of J. Countryman, a division of Thomas Nelson Publishers.

Franklin Graham, excerpted by permission of Thomas Nelson Publishers from the book entitled *All for Jesus* ©2003 Franklin Graham with Ross Rhoads.

Cynthia Heald, excerpted by permission of Thomas Nelson Publishers from the book entitled *Becoming a Woman of Faith* © 2000.

— *Becoming a Woman of Grace* © 1998, excerpted by permission of Thomas Nelson Publishers.

Barbara Johnson, excerpted by permission of W Publishing Group, a division of Thomas Nelson Publishers from the book entitled *The Great Adventure* © 2002.

—*Devotions for a Sensational Life* © 2002, excerpted by permission of Thomas Nelson Publishers.

—*Daily Splashes of Joy* © 2000, excerpted by permission of W Publishing Group, a division of Thomas Nelson Publishers.

—*Irrepressible Hope,* © 2003, excerpted by permission of W Publishing Group, a division of Thomas Nelson Publishers © 2003.

Nicole Johnson, excerpted by permission of W Publishing Group, a division of Thomas Nelson Publishers from the book entitled *Irrepressible Hope* © 2002.

Anne Graham Lotz, excerpted by permission of W Publishing Group, a division of Thomas Nelson Publishers from the book entitled *Just Give Me Jesus* © 2003 by Anne Graham Lotz.

Max Lucado, excerpted by permission of J. Countryman, a division of Thomas Nelson Publishers from the book entitled *Grace for the Moment* © 2002.

—*A Gentle Thunder* © 1995, by Max Lucado, excerpted by permission of W Publishing Group, a division of Thomas Nelson Publishers.

_*Everyday Blessings* © 2004 by Max Lucado, excerpted by permission of J. Countryman, a division of Thomas Nelson Publishers.

—*In the Grip of Grace* © 1996 by Max Lucado, excerpted by permission of W Publishing Group, a division of Thomas Nelson Publishers.

—*Traveling Light for Mothers* © 2002 by Max Lucado, excerpted by permission of W Publishing Group, a division of Thomas Nelson Publishers.

Catherine Marshall, excerpted by permission of J. Countryman, a division of Thomas Nelson Publishers from the book entitled *Moments That Matter* © 2001 by Marshall-LeSourd LLC.

John C. Maxwell, excerpted by permission of J. Countryman, a division of Thomas Nelson Publishers from the book entitled *Leadership*© 2001 by John C. Maxwell.

Robert J. Morgan, excerpted by permission of Thomas Nelson Publishers from the book entitled *Real Stories for the Soul* © 2000 by Robert J. Morgan.

—*Nelson's Annual Preacher's Sourcebook* © 2004 by Robert J. Morgan, by permission of Thomas Nelson Publishers.

—*Nelson's Complete Book of Stories, Illustrations, and Quotes* © 2000 by Robert J. Morgan, by permission of Thomas Nelson Publishers.

Stormie Omartian, excerpted by permission of Thomas Nelson Publishers from the book entitled *Lord I Want to be Whole* © 2001 by Stormie Omartian.

—*Praying God's Will for Your Life* © 2001 by Stormie Omartian.

Purpose for Everyday Living, © 2003, excerpted by permission of Elm Hill Books, a division of Thomas Nelson Publishers.

Reflections from a Mother's Heart, © 2000, excerpted by permission of J. Countryman, a division of Thomas Nelson Publishers.

Paula Rinehart, excerpted by permission of W Publishing Group, a division of Thomas Nelson Publishers from the book entitled *Strong Women, Soft Hearts* © 2001 by Paula Rinehart.

Sister Wisdom, © 2004, excerpted by permission of Elm Hill Books, a division of Thomas Nelson Publishers.

Charles Stanley, excerpted by permission of Thomas Nelson Publishers from the book entitled *On Holy Ground* © 1999 by Charles Stanley.

—*Into His Presence*, © 2000 by Charles Stanley, excerpted by permission of Thomas Nelson Publishers.

Penelope J. Stokes, excerpted by permission of J. Countryman, a division of Thomas Nelson Publishers from the book entitled *Beside A Quiet Stream* © 1999 by Penelope J. Stokes.

Charles R. Swindoll, excerpted by permission of J. Countryman, a division of Thomas Nelson Publishers from the book entitled *Wisdom for the Way*, © 2001 by Charles R. Swindoll.

—*Perfect Trust*, © 2000 by Charles R. Swindoll, Inc., excerpted by permission of J. Countryman, a division Thomas Nelson Publishers.

—*Five Meaningful Minutes a Day*, © 2003 by Charles R. Swindoll, Inc., excerpted by permission of J. Countryman, a division Thomas Nelson Publishers.

Luci Swindoll, excerpted by permission of W Publishing Group, a division of Thomas Nelson Publishers from the book entitled *The Great Adventure* © 2002.

—*Devotions for a Sensational Life* © 2002, excerpted by permission of Thomas Nelson Publishers.

—*You Bring the Confetti, God Brings the Joy* © 1997, excerpted by permission of W Publishing Group, a division of Thomas Nelson Publishers.

—*Irrepressible Hope*, © 2003, excerpted by permission of W Publishing Group, a division of Thomas Nelson Publishers © 2003.

Becky Tirabassi, excerpted by permission of Thomas Nelson Publishers from the book entitled *Let Prayer Change Your Life* © 1990, 1992, 2000 by Becky Tirabassi.

Understanding God's Promises © 2004, excerpted by permission of Thomas Nelson, Inc.

Sheila Walsh, excerpted by permission of W Publishing Group Thomas Nelson Publishers from the book entitled *The Great Adventure* © 2002

—*Irrepressible Hope*, © 2003, excerpted by permission of W Publishing Group, a division of Thomas Nelson Publishers © 2003.

Prayer Requests

Prayers Answered

Prayers Answered

Blessings Received

Thanks Offered

Thanks Offered

Blessings Received

Thanks Offered